Cross Stitch
A to Z Alphabets

2

10

10

10

11

16

20

20

21

22

22

23

Designed by Licia Lewis

An alphabet of favorite things borders

this sweet design featuring a pair of little girls building a sand castle.

Stitch Count = 189w × 223h

FABRIC SIZE
- One 21" × 24" (53.3cm × 61.0cm) piece of 14-ct. Ivory Aida by Zweigart®

DESIGN SIZE
- 11-ct. = 17⅛" × 20¼" (43.5cm × 51.4cm)
- 14-ct. = 13½" × 16" (34.3cm × 40.6cm)
- 16-ct. = 11¾" × 14" (29.8cm × 35.6cm)

INSTRUCTIONS
Center the design and begin stitching. Work cross stitches, half cross stitches, quarter stitches, and turkey stitches with two strands of cotton embroidery floss. Work blended cross stitches, half cross stitches, and quarter cross stitches with one strand of each color listed. Use one strand of cotton embroidery floss to work backstitches and French knots. Use a pressing cloth to carefully iron the needlework from the back before framing as desired.

Turkey stitch: Following the stitch diagram, use two strands of cotton embroidery floss to work turkey stitches, making sure the loops are evenly sized. Cut the loops at the top and brush the ends to fray.

Favorite Things From A to Z Chart Diagram

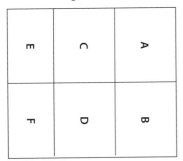

Turkey Stitch

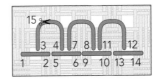

Note: Please read all instructions on page 24 before beginning.

CROSS STITCH

ANCHOR		DMC	COLOR
002	·	White	White
403	X	310	Black
148	A	311	Medium Navy Blue
1017	9	316	Medium Antique Mauve
100	a	327	Dark Violet
013	E	349	Dark Coral
214	T	368	Light Pistachio Green
351	J	400	Dark Mahogany
235	q	414	Dark Steel Gray
943	z	422	Light Hazelnut Brown
832	d	612	Light Drab Brown
891	f	676	Light Old Gold
886	e	677	Very Light Old Gold
228	B	700	Bright Christmas Green
324	w	721	Medium Orange Spice
295	h	726	Light Topaz
280	g	733	Medium Olive Green
304	0	741	Medium Tangerine
301	k	744	Pale Yellow
128	S	775	Very Light Baby Blue
024	1	776	Medium Pink
133	V	796	Dark Royal Blue
131	U	798	Dark Delft Blue
168	K	807	Peacock Blue
023	F	818	Baby Pink
390	8	822	Light Beige Gray
033	D	892	Medium Carnation

CROSS STITCH

ANCHOR		DMC	COLOR
027	b	894	Very Light Carnation
256	O	906	Medium Parrot Green
1003	P	922	Light Copper
881	t	945	Tawny
1011	/	948	Very Light Peach
187	Z	958	Dark Sea Green
185	P	964	Light Sea Green
1001	Q	976	Medium Golden Brown
870	4	3042	Light Antique Violet
129	Y	3325	Light Baby Blue
328	L	3341	Apricot
031	7	3708	Light Melon
1023	6	3712	Medium Salmon
869	J	3743	Very Light Antique Violet
1030	?	3746	Dark Blue Violet
140	5	3755	Baby Blue
1037	R	3756	Ultra Very Light Baby Blue
868	N	3779	Ultra Very Light Terra Cotta
066	C	3806	Light Cyclamen Pink
386	r	3823	Ultra Pale Yellow
5975	H	3830	Medium Terra Cotta

CROSS STITCH WITH BLENDED THREAD

ANCHOR		DMC	COLOR
891	+	676	Light Old Gold
031		3708	Light Melon
304	&	741	Medium Tangerine
129		3325	Light Baby Blue

FRENCH KNOT

ANCHOR		DMC	COLOR
002	●	White	White
403	●	310	Black
033	●	892	Medium Carnation

BACKSTITCH

ANCHOR		DMC	COLOR
403	——	310	Black
148	——	311	Medium Navy Blue
013	——	349	Dark Coral
235	——	414	Dark Steel Gray
310	——	434	Light Brown
178	——	791	Very Dark Cornflower Blue
131	——	798	Dark Delft Blue
152	——	823	Dark Navy Blue
1029	——	915	Dark Plum
187	——	958	Dark Sea Green
905	——	3021	Very Dark Brown Gray
140	——	3775	Baby Blue
1048	——	3776	Light Mahogany

TURKEY STITCH

ANCHOR		DMC	COLOR
002	∩	White	White
228	∩	700	Bright Christmas Green

Bright blue area indicates last row of previous section of design.

TOP

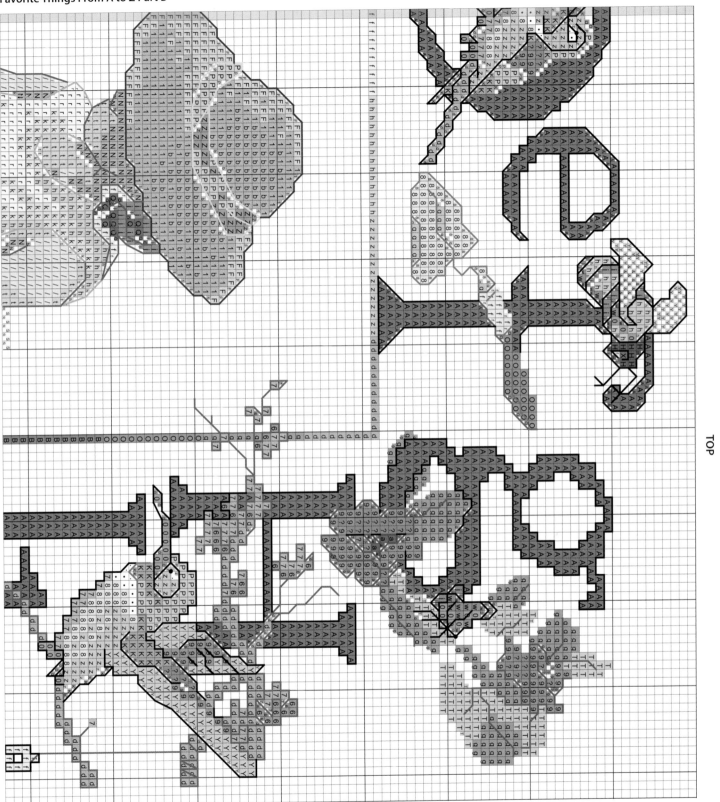

TOP

Note: Color key can be found on page 3.

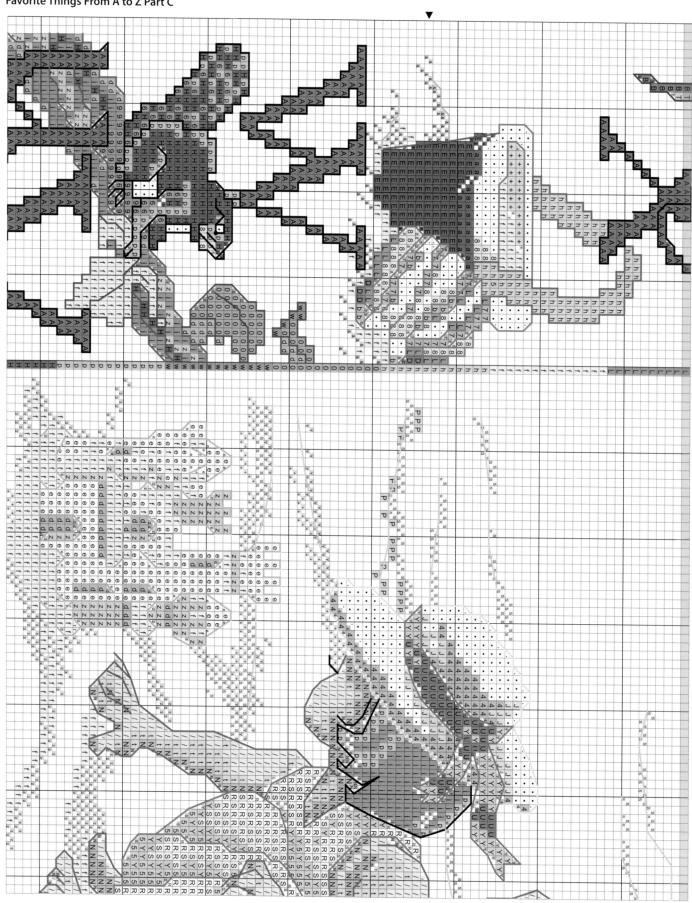

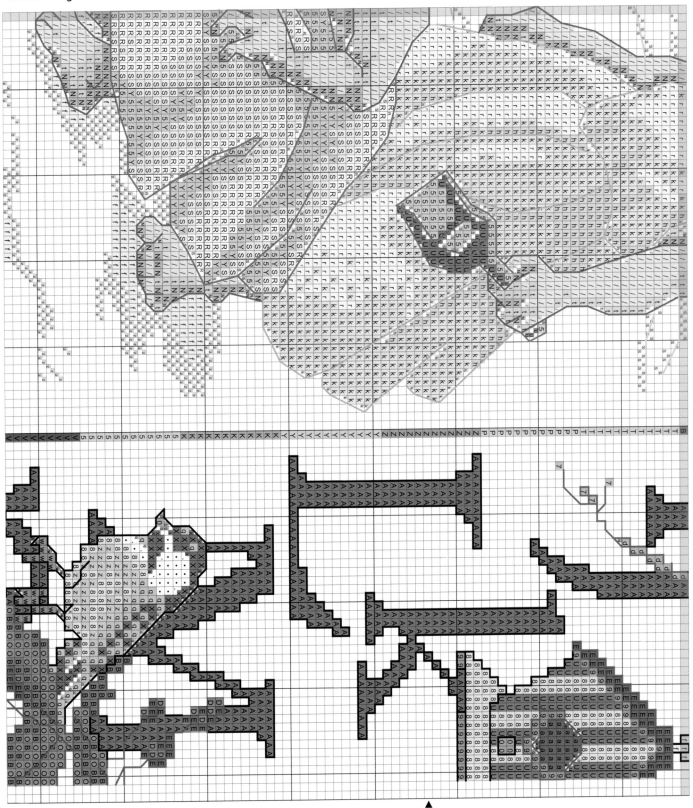

Note: Color key can be found on page 3.

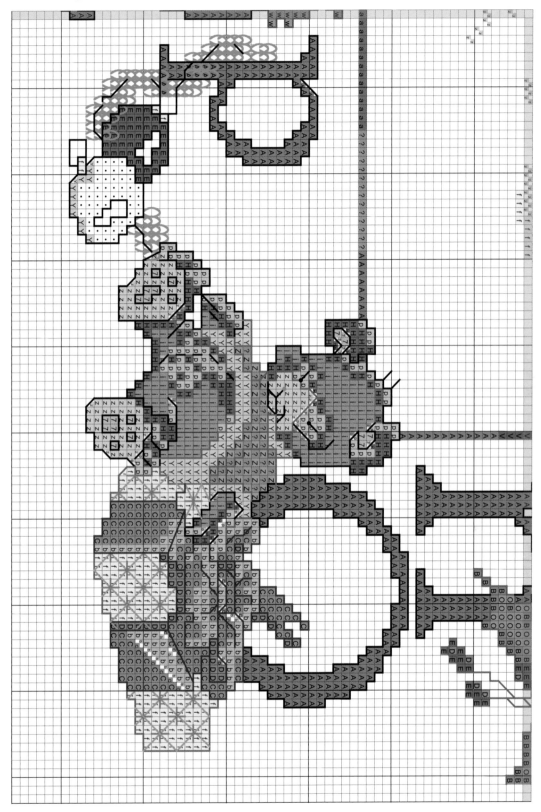

Note: Color key can be found on page 3.

Designed by Alma Lynne Hayden

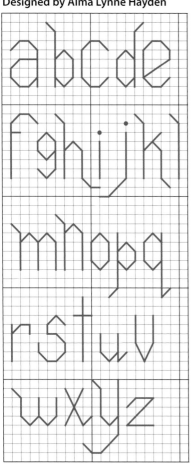

Designed by Michele Johnson

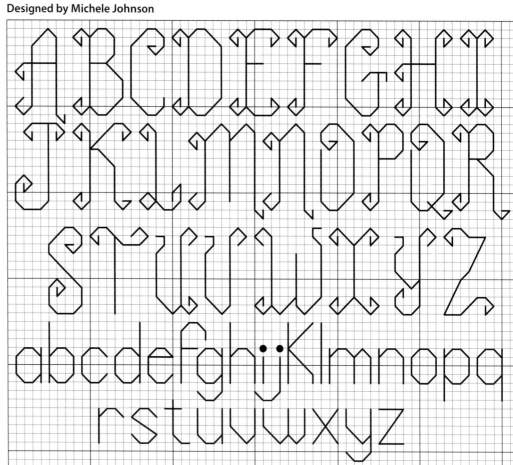

Designed by Cathy Bussi

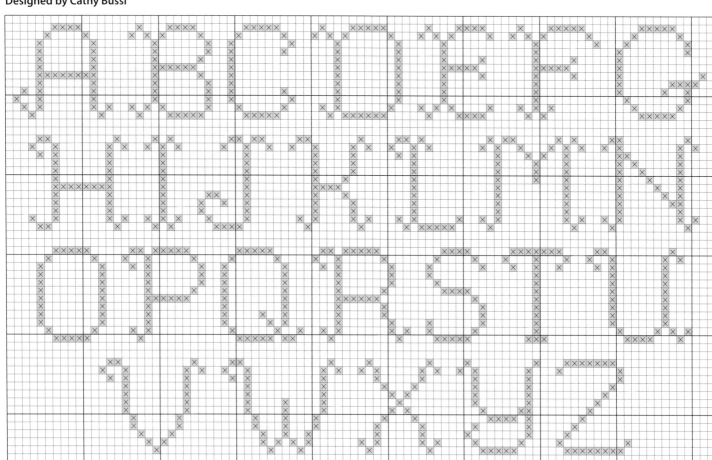

Designed by Sharon Pope

A Is for Apple

Stitch your way through the alphabet with this stunning sampler featuring a motif for each letter.

Note: Please read all instructions on page 24 before beginning.

Stitch Count = 125w × 163h

FABRIC SIZE
- One 17" × 20" (43.2cm × 50.8cm) piece of 28-ct. Sandstone Linen by Wichelt Imports (stitched over two threads)

DESIGN SIZE
- 25-ct. = 10" × 13" (25.4cm × 33.0cm)
- 28-ct. = 8⅞" × 11⅝" (22.5cm × 29.5cm)
- 32-ct. = 7⅞" × 10⅛" (20.0cm × 25.7cm)

INSTRUCTIONS
Center the design and begin stitching over two fabric threads. Work cross stitches, quarter cross stitches, and DMC® 780/Anchor 309 backstitches with two strands of cotton embroidery floss. Use one strand of cotton embroidery floss to work all other backstitches, straight stitches, French knots, and Algerian eyelets. Use a pressing cloth to carefully iron the needlework from the back before framing as desired.

Algerian Eyelet

Note: Color key can be found on pages 14-15.

A Is for Apple Chart Diagram

A	B
C	D

Project Tip

Keeping Fabric Clean in a Hoop
When using a hoop, try putting a sheet of white tissue paper in the hoop on top of the fabric. Tear away the tissue paper in the area where you are stitching. This keeps oils from your hands from getting on the fabric and helps keep the needlework piece free from stains. And whether you use a hoop or not, always wash and dry your hands completely before starting any stitching.

CROSS STITCH

ANCHOR		DMC	COLOR
002	·	White	White
110	6	208	Very Dark Lavender
109	5	209	Dark Lavender
9046	V	321	Christmas Red
011	U	350	Medium Coral
010	8	351	Coral
009	7	352	Light Coral
310	4	434	Light Brown
1045	3	436	Tan
267	E	469	Avocado Green
266	T	470	Light Avocado Green
1005	W	498	Dark Christmas Red
8581	1	646	Dark Beaver Gray
1040	A	647	Medium Beaver Gray
900	Y	648	Light Beaver Gray

A Is for Apple Part D

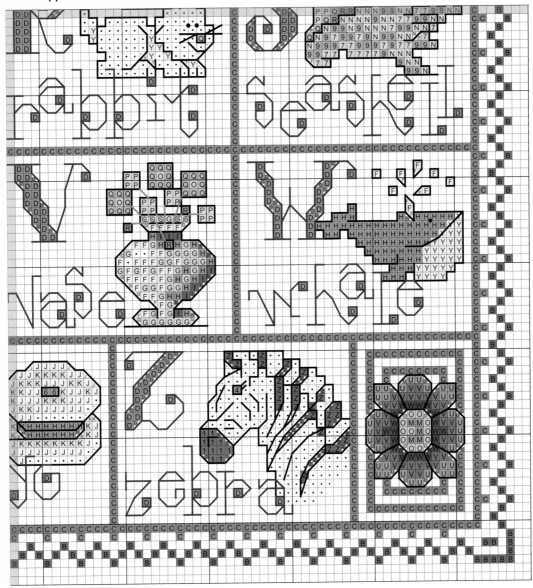

CROSS STITCH

ANCHOR		DMC	COLOR
305	O	725	Medium Light Topaz
295	K	726	Light Topaz
293	J	727	Very Light Topaz
361	2	738	Very Light Tan
1012	N	754	Light Peach
882	9	758	Very Light Terra Cotta
309	B	780	Ultra Very Dark Topaz
308	D	782	Dark Topaz
307	M	783	Medium Topaz
161	F	813	Light Blue
164	I	824	Very Dark Blue
162	H	825	Dark Blue
161	G	826	Medium Blue
1003	S	921	Copper
268	C	937	Medium Avocado Green

CROSS STITCH

ANCHOR		DMC	COLOR
076	R	961	Dark Dusty Rose
075	Q	962	Medium Dusty Rose
073	L	963	Ultra Very Light Dusty Rose
905	Z	3021	Very Dark Brown Gray
025	P	3716	Very Light Dusty Rose

FRENCH KNOT

ANCHOR		DMC	COLOR
9046	•	321	Christmas Red
266	•	470	Light Avocado Green
305	•	725	Medium Light Topaz
309	•	780	Ultra Very Dark Topaz
307	•	783	Medium Topaz
161	•	826	Medium Blue
076	•	961	Dark Dusty Rose
905	•	3021	Very Dark Brown Gray

BACKSTITCH

ANCHOR		DMC	COLOR
900	—	648	Light Beaver Gray
309	—	780	Ultra Very Dark Topaz
307	—	783	Medium Topaz
905	—	3021	Very Dark Brown Gray

STRAIGHT STITCH

ANCHOR		DMC	COLOR
266	—	470	Light Avocado Green

ALGERIAN EYELET

ANCHOR		DMC	COLOR
307	✳	783	Medium Topaz
076	✳	961	Dark Dusty Rose

Part B

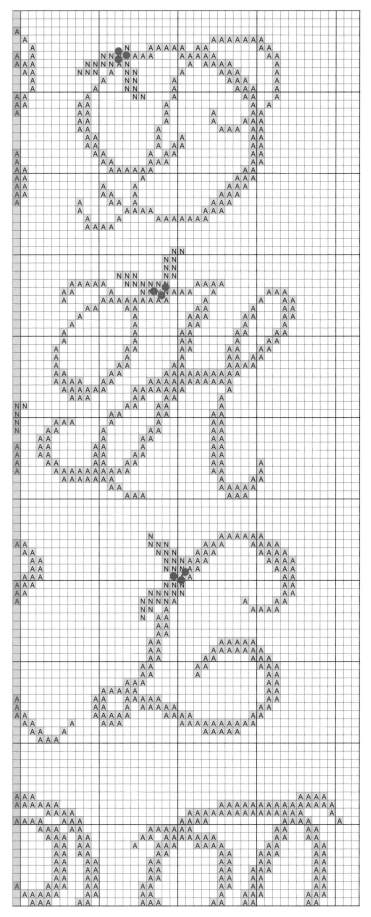

CROSS STITCH

ANCHOR	DMC	COLOR
1006	A 304	Medium Christmas Red
280	N 733	Medium Olive Green

BEAD

MILL HILL GLASS SEED	COLOR
00123 ●	Cream

Mitchell Chart Diagram

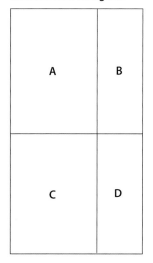

Project Tip

Prevent Twisting
During the movement of stitching, the needle naturally twists, which can cause loops and knots in the thread. To prevent this, work several stitches, then make note of which way the thread unwinds when you hang it straight down from your work. Give your needle a partial turn in that direction with each stitch to keep the thread from twisting.

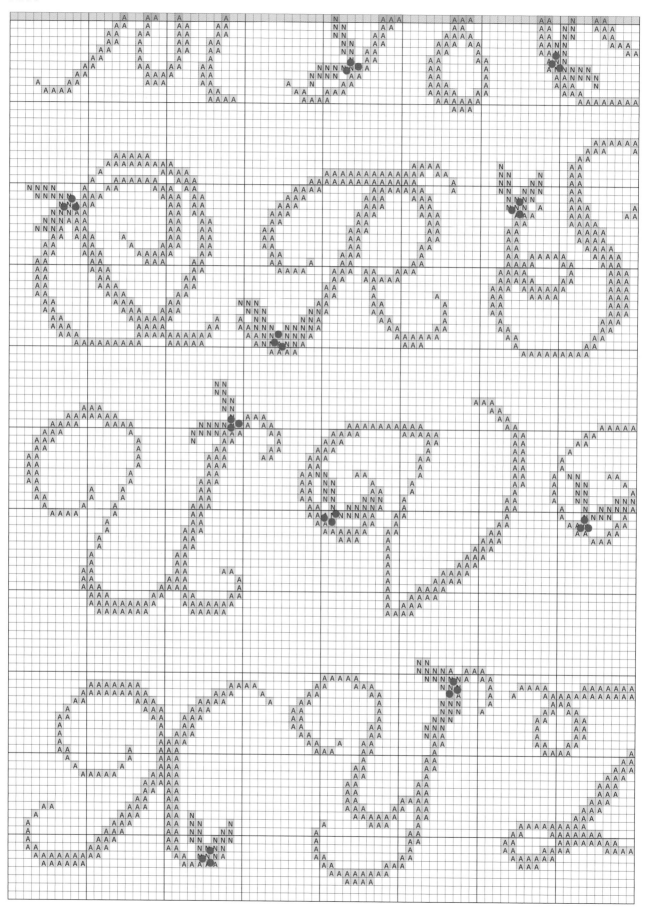

Part D

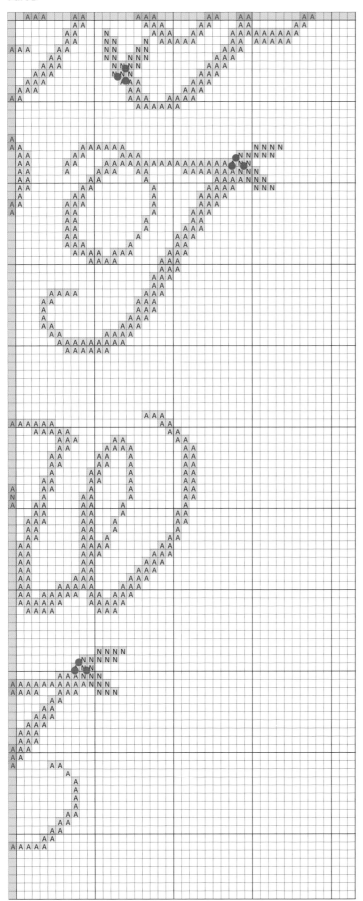

CROSS STITCH

ANCHOR		DMC	COLOR
1006	A	304	Medium Christmas Red
280	N	733	Medium Olive Green

BEAD

MILL HILL GLASS SEED		COLOR
00123	●	Cream

Project Tip

Go With the Grain

Embroidery floss comes in a twisted length made up of six strands that must be separated before stitching can begin. Even though the floss looks perfectly uniform, it does have a grain. By following the grain you lessen the wear and tear on your thread as you draw it through the fabric. This results in stitches that look smoother and silkier. To find the grain direction, cut a length of floss. Loop the thread over so both the cut ends lie next to each other. Do not allow the two ends to bundle together as you must be able to differentiate between them. Holding the cut lengths close together, about ½" from the tips, use one finger of your free hand to gently tap the cut ends. Watch carefully—the end that balloons most is the end that should be threaded through your needle (and is the shorter tail). This tiny extra step can make a significant difference to the look of your finished stitching!

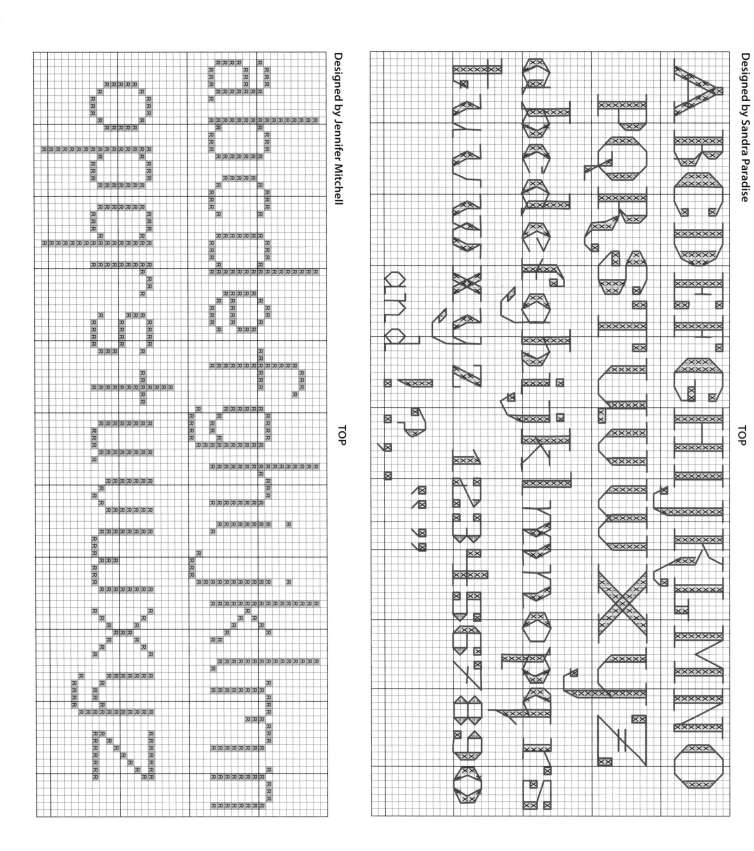

Designed by Sandra Paradise

TOP

Designed by Jennifer Mitchell

TOP

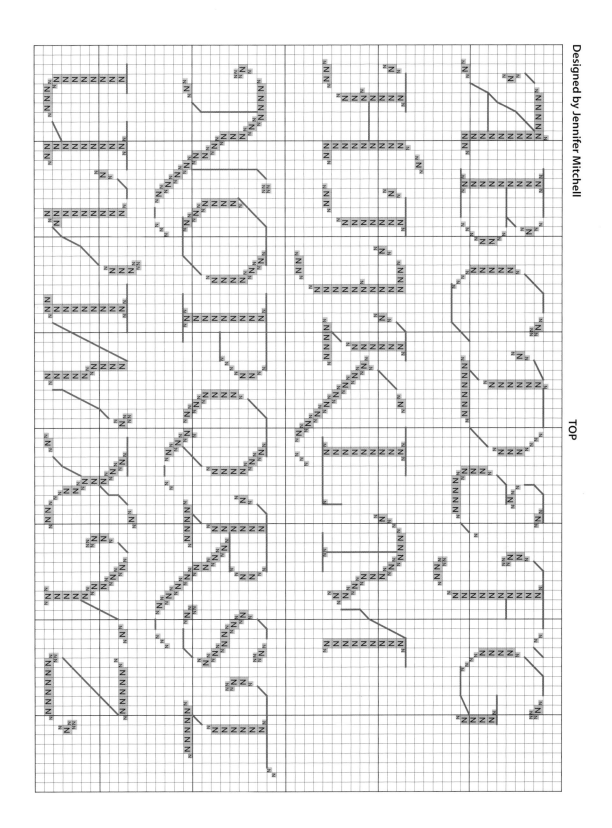

TOP

TOP

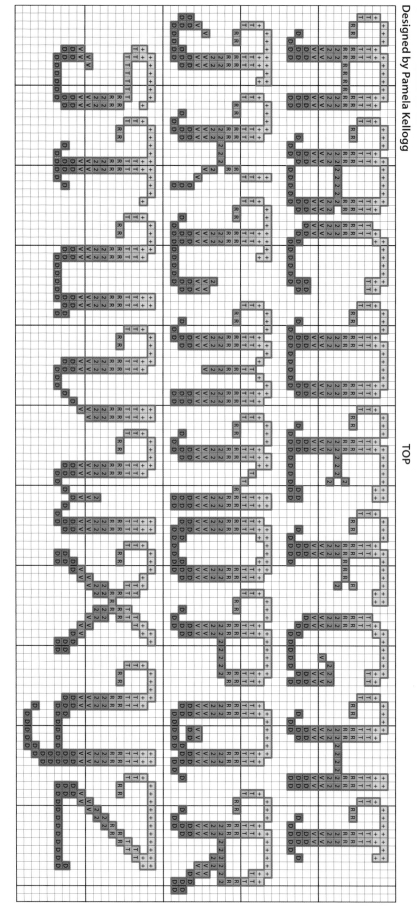

CROSS STITCH

ANCHOR		DMC	COLOR
259	+	772	Very Light Yellow Green
1044	D	895	Very Dark Hunter Green
268	M	3345	Dark Hunter Green
267	2	3346	Hunter Green
266	R	3347	Medium Yellow Green
264	T	3348	Light Yellow Green

BACKSTITCH

	COLOR
KREINIK #4 BRAID	
002 —	Gold

Designed by Elizabeth Spurlock   TOP

A B C D E F G H I J K L M N
O P Q R S T U V W X Y Z
a b c d e f g h i j k l m n
o p q r s t u v w x y z
1 2 3 4 5 6 7 8 9 0

Designed by Barbara Sestok

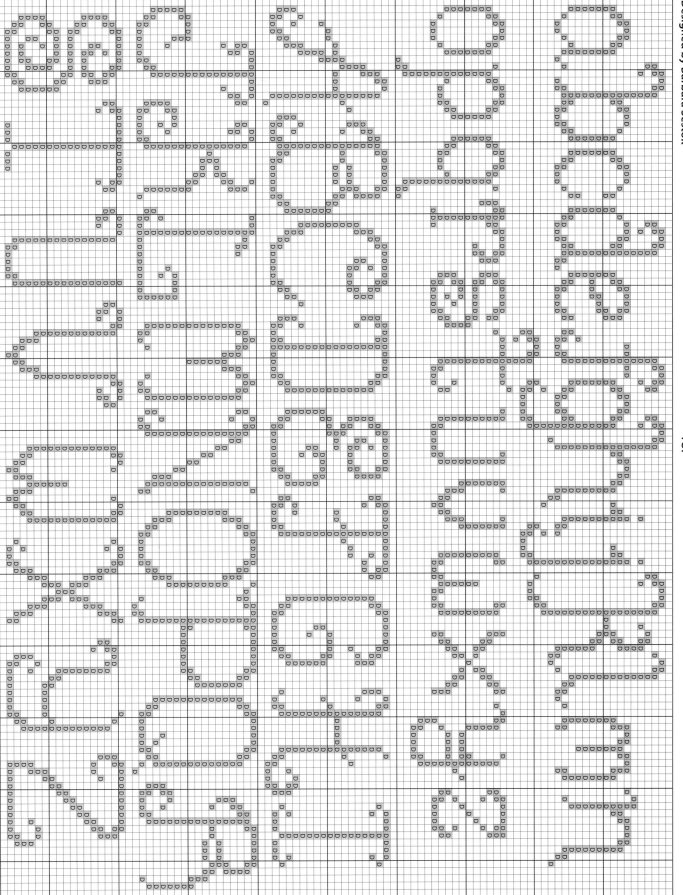

TOP

Getting Started

Cut the floss into 15" lengths and separate all six strands. Recombine the appropriate number of strands and thread them into a blunt-tip needle.

Unless otherwise indicated, cross stitches, three-quarter cross stitches, half cross stitches, and quarter cross stitches are worked with two strands of floss, and backstitches, straight stitches, and French knots with one strand. For lettering that consists of backstitches only, use two strands of floss if you prefer thicker lettering. Work stitches over one thread if stitching on aida and over two threads if stitching on linen or evenweave.

To Secure Thread at the Beginning

The most common way to secure the beginning tail of the thread is to hold it on the wrong side of the fabric under the first four or five stitches.

To Secure Thread at the End

To finish, slip the threaded needle under previously stitched threads on the wrong side of the fabric for four or five stitches, weaving the thread back and forth a few times. Clip the thread.

Personalizing Designs

You can use the alphabets to stitch just a name, monogram, or date, or you can incorporate the letters into part of another stitched design.

To personalize a piece of fabric or a larger design, begin by counting the stitchable area you have to work with (stitches wide by stitches high). Mark this area on a piece of graph paper. Find the center of the stitchable area and the center of the name or monogram—this will determine if a letter or a space will be at the center.

Begin charting the name or monogram onto the graph paper, centering the middle letter or space and working outward. Use a pencil for this, as you may need to adjust the spacing so as to best utilize the area. In most cases, one or two empty rows between letters will work best, but some thin letters (I, L, T, etc.) may look better with more empty rows around them. Be consistent, and make sure the name or monogram looks even and balanced.

Match up the center of the fabric to the center of your graphed letters. Begin stitching at the center and work out to be sure the lettering is centered correctly on the fabric.

Cross Stitch

Make one cross stitch for each symbol on the chart. For horizontal rows, stitch the first diagonal of each

stitch in the row. Work back across the row, completing each stitch. On most linen and evenweave fabrics, work the stitches over two threads as shown in the diagram. For aida cloth, each stitch fills one square. You also can work cross stitches in the reverse direction. Remember to embroider the stitches uniformly—that is, always work the top half of each stitch in the same direction.

Quarter and Three-Quarter Cross Stitches

To obtain rounded shapes in a design, use quarter and three-quarter cross stitches. On linen and evenweave fabrics, a quarter

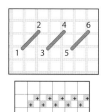

stitch will extend from the corner to the center intersection of the threads. To make quarter cross stitches on aida cloth, estimate the center of the square. Three-quarter cross stitches combine a quarter cross stitch with a half cross stitch. Both stitches may slant in any direction.

Half Cross Stitch

A half cross stitch is a single diagonal or half a cross stitch. They are indicated on the chart by a diagonal colored symbol.

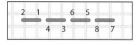

Backstitch

Bring the needle up from the back side of the fabric at odd numbers and

go down at even numbers. Continue, keeping all the stitches the same length.

French Knot

Bring the threaded needle through the fabric and wrap the floss around the needle as shown. Tighten the twists and return the needle through the fabric in the same place. The floss will slide through the wrapped thread to make the knot.

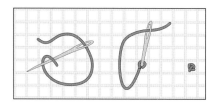

Straight Stitch

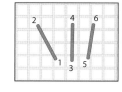

Bring the needle up from the back side of the fabric, then bring the needle down through the fabric in the desired spot to make a stitch of the desired length.

Project Ideas

- Create personalized stocking holders for each member of your family by inserting your needlework into a frame stocking holder that has an opening large enough to fit your stitching.

- Accent a present with a gift tag.

- Create personalized handkerchiefs by stitching initials in the corner of the fabric.

- Use the alphabets to create your own greeting cards. Chart a saying on graph paper, such as "Greetings," "Thank You," or "Congratulations." Then stitch the saying on fabric and insert the piece into a greeting card with a photo opening. (Before stitching your saying, be sure the stitched piece will fit in the photo opening.)

- Don't limit yourself to cotton embroidery floss and aida or evenweave— try different fibers and fabrics, such as tapestry wool, metallic braid, plastic canvas, perforated paper, or needlepoint canvas.

Produced by Herrschners, Inc., for distribution exclusively by Leisure Arts, Inc., 104 Champs Blvd., STE 100, Maumelle, AR 72113-6738, leisurearts.com.